A Pilgrims Cabin

A Pistol

A Musket

A Cutlass

A Shallop

The Mayflower

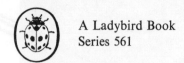

A Ladybird Book
Series 561

Everyone has heard of the Pilgrim Fathers: but who were they? This book tells their story: how men, women and children were crowded in a little wooden ship for more than nine weeks, daring the winter storms of the Atlantic to seek freedom in an unknown land; enduring near-starvation and bitter weather to found a settlement which later grew and spread to become the United States of America.

The
PILGRIM FATHERS

by L. DU GARDE PEACH,
M.A., Ph.D., D.Litt.

with illustrations
by JOHN KENNEY

Publishers: Ladybird Books Ltd . Loughborough
© Ladybird Books Ltd (formerly Wills & Hepworth Ltd) 1972
Printed in England

THE PILGRIM FATHERS

Everybody has heard of the Pilgrim Fathers, the brave men and women who sailed across the Atlantic in a little storm-driven ship in the year 1620. The Pilgrim Fathers went to America to escape religious persecution at home after the Scottish King James VI had succeeded Queen Elizabeth as James I of England.

They are the best remembered of all the American colonists, but they were not the first. After the discovery of America by Columbus in 1492, the Pope had granted the whole of the country to the Spaniards. The fact that it did not belong to him, and that he had no right to grant it to anyone, did not seem to matter. Only five years later John Cabot sailed from Bristol and discovered Newfoundland. He returned to England to report rich fishing grounds off the island, and was generously rewarded by King Henry VII with the handsome sum of ten pounds.

It was the Spaniards who first founded a colony in America but they were not true colonists. All they cared for was to get the gold and silver, in which metals they believed the new lands to be rich.

The Portuguese followed closely upon the Spaniards, and in 1562 a party of French Protestants also arrived to settle in what is now Florida. They, like the Spaniards, were also unsatisfactory colonists, too lazy even to catch the plentiful fish in the rivers at their doors. Under attack by both the natives and the Spaniards, it is not surprising that this attempt to found a French colony failed miserably.

  0 7214 0316 6

The Spaniards looked upon anyone else as trespassers, and when later they attacked and captured a French settlement, they showed no mercy. All the French settlers were hanged on the branches of nearby trees. But so as not to provoke the French nation, the Spaniards pinned a notice to each victim saying that they had been executed "not as Frenchmen, but as Protestants". The French sent an expedition, captured the Spaniards, and hanged them all from the same branches. To each Spaniard they pinned a notice saying that they were hanged "not as Spaniards, but as murderers!"

In the year 1578 Queen Elizabeth granted a charter to a famous English sailor, Sir Humphrey Gilbert. This charter gave him permission "to inhabit and possess at his choice all heathen lands not in the possession of any Christian peoples." Five years later, in 1583, Sir Humphrey Gilbert landed on the island of Newfoundland with some two hundred men. With him was his young half-brother, Walter Raleigh.

The colony was not successful, and Sir Humphrey Gilbert was drowned on the return voyage to England. Walter Raleigh was not discouraged by the disastrous end to the enterprise. With another and smaller company he landed on another island, Roanoke, and named the new colony Virginia in honour of the Queen. When this failed, further attempts were made, but with little success.

A more promising colonial enterprise was interrupted by greater events. The year was 1588, and in Spanish shipyards a great fleet was being built to sail against England: it was the Spanish Armada. The colonisation of America was for a time largely postponed. Thirty-two years later the Pilgrim Fathers landed on the mainland of North America.

Who were these Pilgrim Fathers who were ready to face the dangers which awaited them in an almost unknown land, inhabited by strange natives and denied to them by the Spaniards? To answer this question we must go back to the reign of Elizabeth.

Under Good Queen Bess, the affectionate name bestowed on Elizabeth by the people, England was a Protestant Country. Queen Mary, her elder sister who was a Catholic, had persecuted the Protestants: now they in their turn began to persecute the Catholics. King Henry VIII, Elizabeth's father, had established the Church of England, and most English citizens were content with an English Church governed by bishops appointed by the Crown. But some of the Protestants, known as Puritans, thought that the bishops of the Church of England were too much like the Catholic bishops by whom they had been persecuted. These people were given the name of Puritans because they wanted to purify, or reform, the Church by getting rid of the bishops, together with much of the ceremonial of the Church Service.

In those days the Church and the reigning King or Queen were the two ruling powers of the country. Neither could hope successfully to govern without the help of the other. Elizabeth felt that it was her duty to put down the Puritans as a danger to the Established Church.

This was often done very harshly, even though most of the Puritans only asked to be left alone to worship God in their own way. They were neither wicked nor criminal, but they were frequently treated as though they were both. Men were dragged from their homes and imprisoned or made to stand in the pillory; women were separated from their children; few escaped some shameful form of punishment.

Queen Elizabeth had said that she "made no windows into men's souls". She meant that they could think as they liked, so long as they kept quiet about it. This the Puritans were not prepared to do, and they saw no hope of any real religious freedom in England. Under James I things became more difficult still, and a number of extreme Puritans determined to leave the country for ever.

The problem was where to go? Countries such as France, Spain, and Italy were Catholic and closed to them. There remained the northern countries of Europe. The Puritans looked hopefully across the North Sea to find a place to live free from religious persecution.

There were many small groups of Puritans living in various parts of England. The one from which the Pilgrim Fathers came was originally founded at Gainsborough, in Lincolnshire, about 1602, one year before Queen Elizabeth died. Four years later some of the members of this group moved to the small village of Scrooby in Nottinghamshire, two miles south of Bawtry on the Great North Road. This was what was called a posting station, where the horses of the coaches were changed. The man in charge of it was one of the Puritans, William Brewster.

Two other members of this congregation of Puritans were John Robinson, a university graduate and formerly a clergyman of the Church of England, and William Bradford, who later became the Governor of the new colony in America. The Puritans could only meet secretly, and the congregation gathered in Scrooby Manor House. When it became necessary for their safety to leave England, it was here that many anxious meetings must have taken place.

Even today, it is sometimes difficult for people to leave a country without permission, especially a country in which they are being persecuted. This was the position of the Puritans of Scrooby. When they decided to go to Holland, known also as the Netherlands, they had to be smuggled secretly out of England.

Holland was a Protestant country, and already some English Protestants had found refuge there. The men and women from Scrooby felt that they would be amongst friends. What was more important, they would not be persecuted because of their religion.

First they had to arrange for a ship. Soon, after some difficulty, a ship was waiting for them at Boston, in Lincolnshire. It was fifty miles away as the crow flies, but they had to follow unfrequented lanes and cart-tracks. A party of Protestants travelling along the main roads, such as they were in those days, would almost certainly be arrested. The distance they had to travel was sixty or seventy miles, and every weary mile had to be covered on foot.

They must have been very travel-worn by the time they reached Boston. When they saw the little ship waiting to take them to freedom, they imagined that their troubles were over. They were wrong. The captain of the ship was a scoundrel who was only waiting to get them aboard, before handing them all over to the authorities. They were immediately arrested and some of them imprisoned. But they were determined to escape. When they were released they tried again, this time with a loyal Dutch captain. The picture opposite shows them landing safely in Amsterdam.

Even then their troubles were not at an end. When people live in a free country and are allowed to think and say what they like, there are many things about which they do not all think in the same way. Especially is this the case in matters of religion. When some of these people are what we call intolerant, that is unable to agree to differ in a friendly way, there is certain to be trouble.

The ordinary Protestants and the more extreme Puritans had all left England to obtain religious freedom: now that they had got it, they failed to practise it amongst themselves. Bitter differences of opinion arose. Soon a number of them left the Church at Amsterdam and settled in the Dutch town of Leyden twenty-five miles away. These were the future Pilgrim Fathers.

The people of Leyden were friendly towards the English refugees. A famous University had been founded there thirty years earlier, and there were many liberal-minded men in the town. But although some of the Puritans were skilled craftsmen, they were not always allowed to work at their various trades. This was because of the strict control of the Guilds, much like the Trades Unions of today.

The little group remained in Leyden for ten years. But they were foreigners in a foreign country. They were not persecuted, and they had complete religious freedom, but it was not enough. Their children were growing up speaking Dutch rather than English, and were in danger of losing all contact with their native land. Emigration to the New World appeared to be the only solution.

There were already a few small, scattered settlements on the east coast of North America. One of these was in Virginia, and it was decided by the Puritans at Leyden that the best thing to do would be to join them. To settle in Virginia it was necessary to obtain permission from the King of England. Fortunately the Puritans had some friends in London of sufficient social importance to claim an audience with King James. The King saw no reason why he should grant permission for Puritans, whom he disliked, to settle in lands claimed by England. "How are they going to live?" he is said to have asked. "By fishing," was the reply. "It's an honest trade: it was the calling of the Apostles themselves," replied the King, and granted permission.

It was a very small group which at the end of July, in the year 1620, embarked in a little ship of sixty tons at a Dutch port. In this ship they sailed to Southampton. At Southampton the *Speedwell*, which had brought them safely from Holland, joined the famous *Mayflower*. Here also they found a party of about ninety emigrants bound like themselves for America.

It may seem strange that the Puritans, who ten years earlier had been smuggled out of England, could return openly without being arrested. But they were now under the protection of powerful friends at court, and had the King's permission. This made all the difference.

There were however, other difficulties. The Puritans were godly people, quiet, sober, and deeply religious. The emigrants, whom they joined at Southampton, were very different. They were most of them very poor, and no doubt some of them had good reasons, far from religious, for getting out of England.

The party of emigrants at Southampton must have thought that the Puritans were very queer people. They seemed always to be praying or singing hymns. The ninety emigrants did neither, and it appeared very doubtful whether the two parties could ever work peacefully together.

There were other and more immediate troubles. The *Speedwell* had safely crossed the North Sea, but no sooner did she reach rougher waters than her captain complained that she was leaking badly. He said that it would be very dangerous to attempt to reach America in her. The two ships put back first into Dartmouth and then into Plymouth.

Here they were told that the *Speedwell* was beyond immediate repair. There was really nothing wrong with her, but the cowardly captain was afraid of the voyage into unknown seas. It was decided that the *Mayflower* should sail alone, and as many went aboard as the little ship would hold. She set sail from Plymouth at the beginning of September, 1620.

She was very small, even for those days. We must picture a little sailing ship of 180 tons, with two masts carrying square sails. She had also a small mast aft with a three-cornered sail set at an angle, called a lateen sail. She was less than 100 feet long, and had been in the wine trade. There was no cabin accommodation for the hundred or so pilgrims on board. They slept, ate and lived wherever they could find room during the nine weeks, many of them stormy, at sea. It must have been very uncomfortable indeed. At one point the captain wanted to turn back, but in spite of sea-sickness and accidents, the brave Pilgrim Fathers insisted on continuing the voyage.

In addition to the discomforts of the voyage, there was trouble between the Puritans and the emigrants, who outnumbered the party from Leyden and wanted to take command. The Puritans naturally disagreed. As they were men of character and determination, they soon brought the larger number of emigrants under control.

A meeting was held between the Leyden group and the more responsible of the emigrants, at which a Charter was drawn up for the future government of the colony. From the wording of this Charter it is quite clear by whom it was drafted. Its importance is such that we should read the opening of it in full. It is as follows:

> In the name of God, Amen. WE, having undertaken, for the glory of God, and the advancement of the Christian Faith, a voyage to plant the first colony in the northern parts of Virginia, do by these presents solemnly and mutually in the presence of God and of one another, covenant and combine ourselves together into a civil body politic, for our better ordering and preservation.

The only thing wrong with this document is the name of the place where the colony was ultimately to be founded. In those days navigation was far from being an exact science. Once a captain had been a few days out of sight of land, he had little idea of his position. The *Mayflower* was far off course. The original landing place was planned for the northern part of Virginia, on the Hudson River, near what is now New York. When land was at last sighted, they were nearly 300 miles to the north of it.

It appeared afterwards that the reason for this supposed mistake in navigation was not quite as simple as it seemed. Captain Jones, who commanded the *Mayflower* was the third captain to deceive the Pilgrim Fathers. The Dutch also wished to establish a settlement on the Hudson River, and they had persuaded and probably bribed Captain Jones to make his landing far to the north of it.

The Pilgrim Fathers knew nothing of this at the time. Being themselves incapable of deceit, they believed what they were told. Captain Jones agreed to sail down the coast to the south, to the originally planned destination of the voyage. But they had not been more than half a day on their course when, in the words of one of them, "we fell amongst shoals and breakers, and conceived ourselves in great danger. The next day, being brought safe to land, we fell upon our knees and blessed God, who had delivered us from many perils and miseries".

They were delivered from more perils than they knew. A later settlement in northern Virginia was at the mercy of savage Red Indians: the part of North America where the Pilgrims now found themselves was largely free from this danger. Many of the natives had lately died of a mysterious disease and the rest had moved away.

On November 9th 1620, a party of well-armed men landed from the ship to reconnoitre the country. They found neither inhabitants nor any sign of human habitation. They brought back fresh water and wood for fuel, but decided to search further for a place in which to build a permanent settlement.

It was an uninviting coast off which the *Mayflower* was anchored. The tangled woods came down to a rocky beach, and the Pilgrims imagined all sorts of horrors to be hidden amongst the trees. They had expected to find primitive savages, and they had heard stories of wild animals seen or imagined by colonists further south.

The next few weeks were spent in exploring up and down the coast. Parties of armed men went ashore almost daily. Taking every precaution against possible attack, they cautiously made their way inland. By the 16th of November Captain Jones was growing impatient. He was anxious to get rid of the Pilgrims and the emigrants who were still on board, and he urged them to look more diligently for a place of settlement.

The usual well-armed party again went ashore. Suddenly they saw five Red Indians who ran away into the woods. The party of Pilgrims followed, but was not able to come up with them. Determined to follow the trail of the Indians the next morning, they lit a fire and camped for the night.

We may be sure that they set sentinels to keep strict watch. They knew that the Indians they had seen would warn the rest of the tribe of the arrival of strange white men, and they had no wish to be murdered in their sleep. Nothing happened however, and the next morning they found and followed the tracks of the natives in the snow. At last they came to a place where the land had been cleared, near a pool of fresh water. New stubble, where corn had been cut, seemed to show that an Indian village could not be far away.

Soon they came across the remains of a primitive house and Indian-woven baskets filled with corn, the like of which they had never seen before. There was also a large kettle which the party took back to the ship, together with some of the corn.

All this encouraged them to seek further, and on December 6th, a further reconnaissance was made. In an open boat they sailed along the coast in bitterly cold weather, braving the spray which froze on their coats. As one of them said, they looked as though they had been glazed. They had sight of ten or twelve Indians ashore, but because of the rocks and the breakers they were unable to get near enough to speak with them.

The next day they divided into two parties, one party coasting along in the boat, the other on land following the edge of the water. They found no Indians, nor any place which seemed suitable for a settlement. Determined not to return to the ship until they were successful, they decided to camp for a second night.

Because of the near presence of Indians, they built a barricade of logs and lay down to sleep. Their rest was rudely disturbed. The winter dawn was just breaking when they heard strange and terrible yells. This was the Indian war-whoop, which none of them had ever heard before. Arrows began to fly about them, and they could see the Indians dodging amongst the trees. A volley from the muskets of the armed party soon put their attackers to flight, but still the arrows came. Then they saw that one Indian, braver than the rest, was half hidden behind a tree, sending arrow after arrow against them.

The Indian brave had loosed off several arrows when one of the armed party fired and hit the tree behind which the Indian was taking cover. The splinters flew about his head. With a defiant war-whoop he ran to join his fellows.

The party of Pilgrims, together with some of the crew from the *Mayflower*, continued to sail along the coast. Their troubles were by no means over. The wind got up and the waves increased: it was snowing and bitterly cold. At this point the rudder broke. Two of the sailors managed to steer the boat by using two oars, but soon it became dark and the storm got worse. The waves were driving the boat towards the rocky shore when suddenly the mast, with its rag of storm-sail, broke into three pieces and fell overboard.

Destruction seemed certain. But by hard rowing they managed to get into the lee of a little island where the sea was calmer. Here they anchored for the night.

They had no means of knowing that here they were safe from the Indians. In the darkness and the driving snow it was impossible to tell where they were. Thinking that they were still on the mainland, they landed and lit a large fire. Soon, as one of them wrote afterwards, "the whole were refreshed and rested in safety that night". But the search for a site for permanent settlement was not yet over. Finally after perils and hardships which would have daunted most men, they found what they were seeking. They sailed back to the *Mayflower* with the news, and on December 16th, 1620, their ship anchored off the site of their new-found home.

They were not the first white men to land on this stretch of the coast. The harbour had been roughly mapped in 1608 by Champlain, and in 1614 a certain Captain Smith had named it Plymouth. After thoroughly exploring the immediately surrounding country, the Pilgrims decided that this was the place in which to build their settlement.

On December 21st they landed on the historic Plymouth Rock. This is one of the most famous first landing places in the history not only of the United States of America but of the world. The Rock is still preserved and treasured because on it a party of poor outcasts from the Old World took their first steps in the New World.

It was mid-winter, and winter in North America was no milder then than it is now. The settlers could not remain in the *Mayflower* indefinitely, and the first thing to be done was to construct shelter on shore for themselves and their goods. On Christmas Day, 1620, they began the building of a storehouse.

Houses for men, women and children were the next most urgent need. In the bitter, wintry weather these had to be built quickly as they cleared the snow from one patch after another. A few upright logs roughly fastened together, and roofed with branches covered over with turf, was the best they could do. Oiled paper over holes for windows, and unshaped stones piled together to contain a fire, gave a little light and warmth. It must have been very cheerless and uncomfortable. But the Pilgrim Fathers were prepared to face discomfort and danger in order to be free to live their own lives in their own way.

It was a terrible winter. By the end of March the last of the Pilgrims had come ashore, and by that time some sort of shelter had been built for those who had survived.

These were far fewer in number than those who had left England so hopefully in September. Disease due to lack of good food, and the conditions in which they were forced to live and work, had reduced their numbers to scarce fifty persons. During January and February sometimes as many as three died in a day. Of those who lived, there were often only six or seven well enough to care for the others.

The sailors of the *Mayflower* also suffered, and when in April the ship sailed for England, it was with a very depleted crew. The Pilgrim Fathers, and the colonists who had crossed the Atlantic with them, were now completely cut off from any contact with civilisation. A week later the man whom they had chosen to be their leader, died whilst working in the fields.

The Pilgrims chose William Bradford to be the new Governor and to watch over the affairs of the little colony. His life had been very sad. When the *Mayflower* sailed from England, he and his wife had been obliged to leave their young son behind, and in December his wife was drowned whilst he was away with one of the early exploring parties. He was a devoted leader. In caring for the fortunes of the settlement he proved to be a wise one as well. His name is remembered and honoured.

In the meantime something of very great importance to the settlement had happened: friendly contact had been made with the Red Indians.

For weeks, as they worked to build their poor huts, the Pilgrims had seen groups of natives in the distance, but when they tried to speak with them, they always ran away into the woods. Then, about the middle of March, an Indian brave came into the settlement.

The Pilgrims stared at him in amazement. With his painted face and feathered head-dress, he was something which up to now they had never seen at close quarters. They were even more amazed when in broken English he bade them welcome and told them that his name was Samoset.

His story was a strange one. He had been taken aboard, some time before, by an English skipper fishing off the coast, and had learnt English from the crew. This meant that he not only knew where good fishing was to be found, but could tell the settlers this and a good deal more. From Samoset and other natives they learnt all about planting and harvesting the crop which we call Indian corn. This was later to save them from starvation. They were also shown how to obtain the sweet sap from the maple trees, and how to trap the animals which were plentiful in the forest. The coming of Samoset to the little settlement was one of the most fortunate things which ever happened to it. Without his help and that of other Indians, it is doubtful whether it would have survived. The Pilgrims gave thanks to God who, they believed, had sent this help in their time of great need.

When he left, he said he would return with others of his tribe, bringing skins for trade. The Pilgrims watched anxiously, wondering whether he had been a spy sent to find out their weakness so that the Indians might attack them.

Their fears were soon dispelled when Samoset reappeared with five other braves, laden with the skins of deer and beaver. As beaver skins were very valuable in England, the Pilgrims saw the opportunity for profitable trade and offered to take as many of them as the Indians could supply. Samoset sent the braves back for more skins, and remained himself in the settlement. When after some days the party had not returned, the Pilgrims suggested that he should go and look for them.

It was then that their fears returned. Painted faces appeared and vanished amongst the undergrowth in the forest. War-cries and wild yells were heard in the night. The Pilgrims kept watch with loaded muskets, fully expecting to be attacked. Their relief when Samoset returned with another Indian may well be imagined.

Relief turned to amazement when the second Indian spoke English even better than Samoset. His name was Squanto, and he had actually lived for a time in England. He was the last surviving member of the tribe which had originally lived where the Pilgrims had made their settlement. Whilst he had been away the whole tribe had died from disease. In the words of William Bradford, "he was a special instrument sent of God for their good beyond their expectations". Squanto remained with the Pilgrims to interpret between them and the Indians.

Samoset told the Pilgrims about another Indian, a great chief named Massasoiet. He was the chief of a tribe which inhabited a part of the country about forty miles away. Samoset suggested that this chief should be invited to the settlement, so that the Pilgrims might make friends with him. As this would greatly relieve their anxieties, the Pilgrims agreed.

On March 22nd 1621, Chief Massasoiet arrived, accompanied by a large party of armed braves. This was a dangerous number of well-armed Indians to admit into the settlement. The Pilgrims took no chances. They put on their armour and loaded their muskets, knowing that the Indians were afraid of the 'fire sticks' as they called them.

Their fears were needless. Massasoiet was only too anxious to be friendly. When it appeared that there would not be enough food in the settlement to entertain so many, the Chief sent some of his braves to kill deer for the feast. Afterwards, a treaty was drawn up with Massasoiet. In it the two parties promised that neither would attack the other, and that if either was attacked by anyone else, each would help the other to defend themselves. Anything stolen from either by the other, was to be returned, and they were always to meet un-armed.

What the Pilgrims did not know was that Massasoiet and his tribe were often at war with a neighbouring tribe. They wanted to make sure that the men with the 'fire sticks' would be on their side. On the whole it was a fair treaty, and was kept by both sides for more than fifty years.

It was a good feast, and for once the Pilgrims had enough to eat. But when the feast was over, and Massasoiet and his braves had gone, the settlers again faced weeks and months of hunger.

With the coming of spring, the Puritans planted the seed of the Indian corn in the way which Samoset and Squanto had shown them. They also sowed some seed which they had brought from England, but the crop was a failure. Probably the seed had gone bad in the damp hold of the *Mayflower* or the rough, unprepared ground was not suitable. Fortunately the Indian corn did better, and as the weather grew warmer, they also found grapes ripening in the sunshine.

Squanto and another young Indian named Hobomok, showed the settlers how to catch fish for food and for fertilising the soil. By midsummer the future began to look brighter for the Pilgrims.

Unfortunately they had trouble with some of the native tribes who resented the coming of the white man, particularly a chief named Corbitant who treacherously tried to kill Squanto and Hobomok. The two Indians had been sent to trade in skins, and to make friends with Corbitant. They returned with the news that the tribe was hostile and was preparing to attack the settlement. The Pilgrims realised that it was necessary to show the natives that although they wished to live at peace with them, they were strong enough to resist attack and to protect their friends. They decided to send a party of armed men to teach the Indians that it would be safer and better to trade with the Pilgrims, rather than to attack them.

An ex-soldier, Captain Miles Standish, had sailed with the Pilgrims in the *Mayflower*, and he now went with fourteen well-armed men to look for Corbitant. They marched into the Indian village without opposition, and surrounded the wigwam in which Corbitant lived. But he had had word of their coming, and had escaped into the forest where it would be impossible to find him.

Three Indians suddenly appeared as Standish and his men took up their position. Thinking that they were about to be attacked, the Pilgrims opened fire and wounded them. Then, instead of leaving them to die, they took the three wounded men back to the settlement, dressed their wounds and nursed them.

This impressed the Indians more than if they had destroyed the whole village. Chiefs from surrounding tribes came to look at the white men who cured their enemies, a thing they would never have dreamed of doing. Even Corbitant made peace with them, though for a long time he was too shy to visit the settlement.

One tribe, the Narragansets, proved less friendly. They sent a messenger to the settlement with a bundle of arrows tied in a snake-skin. Squanto knew what this meant. He warned the Pilgrims that it was a challenge to battle. In reply, the Governor sent the snake-skin back, filled with bullets. He told the messenger to inform the Chief of the Narragansets that if they loved war rather than peace, they could begin when they liked. But, he added, the Pilgrims had done them no wrong. At the same time, the settlement was ready to resist any attack. The Chief very wisely remembered the 'fire sticks', and did nothing.

The Pilgrims had sent a defiant message back to the Chief of the Narragansets, but they still feared that they might be attacked. The settlement was simply a collection of huts, with no kind of protection. It was decided to build a stockade. This was a strong palisade, eleven feet high and a mile in circumference. It took three months to build, but when it was done, the Pilgrims felt safer.

Later, they built a fort on a nearby hill. They had heard of a massacre of the settlers in Virginia by Indians, and were afraid that it might encourage those who lived near them, to try to get rid of the white settlers.

The fort was built on some high ground known as Burial Hill. It was here that Bradford and some of the original settlers were buried. Those who had died during the first terrible winter had no known graves. The ground had been levelled and sown with corn, so that the Indians would not realise how few were left. The new fort was a watch tower, manned whenever danger threatened.

In the meantime the little colony had grown. Exactly a year after the *Mayflower* had cast anchor off Cape Cod, a little ship was sighted by the excited Pilgrims. They had had no contact with civilisation for so long that they eagerly awaited the first boats to come ashore. The ship, of only fifty-five tons, was the *Fortune* and had sailed from London four months earlier. The Pilgrims hoped that it had brought seed-corn and provisions. They were disappointed. The ship had brought thirty-five new settlers, but nothing to help feed them.

When they first sailed for the New World, the Pilgrims had been lent money by a Company in England called the Merchant Adventurers. The *Fortune* brought angry letters from this Company, complaining that no cargo had been sent back in the *Mayflower* to help pay off the debt. This was very unfair. The settlers barely had time to build shelters before they had been left by Captain Jones to shift for themselves.

The Pilgrims worked hard to pay off the debt. They had been cutting the valuable cedar wood and collecting beaver skins. These were now loaded into the *Fortune*, and two weeks after her arrival she sailed for England. But the Pilgrims were again unfortunate. As the little ship was entering the English Channel, she was attacked and captured by a French privateer. All the labour of the settlers was lost.

As no supplies had been sent in the *Fortune*, the Pilgrim Fathers faced near-starvation. They were in this sad state when two more ships arrived, the *Charity* and the *Swan*, with sixty men aboard. They landed, as Governor Bradford recorded, without so much as "a bite of bread". Although they were so short of food themselves, the Pilgrims shared with the new-comers what food they had. They were ill repaid. The sixty men soon moved to a place to the north called Wessagusset. Here they set up a new settlement and a trading post for beaver skins in opposition to the Pilgrims.

The next harvest was poor in both settlements, so it was decided to join forces to trade with the natives. Bradford and Squanto went with the party from Plymouth. Although they were successful in obtaining some beans and corn, it was an unfortunate expedition: poor Squanto died of a fever.

The sixty men in Wassagusset ill-treated the Indians and stole from their crops and store-houses. The natives became understandably hostile and the colony at Wassagusset was abandoned for the time being. But the hard-working, God-fearing Pilgrims remained and prospered. Courage and devotion won where aggression had failed.

The Pilgrims owed much of their success as colonists to their hard work and determination. But they never forgot that though man plants the seed, God sends the harvest. To commemorate their first harvest in the New World they set apart a Day of Thanksgiving as a Festival. It is still observed in the United States on the last Thursday in November. Religious services are held in all the churches, families are reunited, and old friends remembered.

On this day it is a poor table which does not boast a turkey: it is as traditional as the Christmas pudding in England. It's origin is in a story which if not historically true, certainly ought to be.

The first Thanksgiving Day of all was in October, 1621. The Pilgrims decided to invite to their Thanksgiving Feast the Red Indians who had proved their friends. Ample food was provided, but when a hundred warriors arrived, all hungrily eyeing the preparations, their hospitable hosts realised that there would not be enough to go round. The Red Indian Chief saw the look of consternation on their faces. With the consideration of a gentleman, he sent some of his braves into the woods: they returned with enough wild turkeys to feed an army.

Many of the towns and cities of today began as a few huts built by fishermen on some natural harbour, or by pioneers in unexplored country; by refugees from tyranny or by nomadic shepherds seeking fresh pasturage for their flocks. Once established, if the site were well chosen, such communities attracted more immigrants, until ultimately a new town or city was the result.

This is what happened to the little settlement of the Pilgrim Fathers. More fugitives from civil or religious persecution ventured across the Atlantic. Masons and carpenters, architects and artists, writers and musicians sought the opportunities offered by a new life in the New World. As more land was taken over for cultivation, the Indians retreated westwards; scattered settlements grew into prosperous towns; metalled roads replaced rough tracks through the forest. Better houses were built in place of the primitive log cabins, and all the refinements of life to which the newly-arrived colonists had been used in Europe, were gradually introduced into the new towns.

Ten years after the landing of the Pilgrim Fathers a pamphlet was printed asserting, in the spelling of 1630, that "Here are strawberries and raspberries, currance and plums, cowcombers and pumpions bigger and sweeter than in England". Every variety of fruit and vegetable, including "aboundance of sweet Hearbes delightful to the smell, whose names we know not," made an attractive picture.

New Plymouth became a thriving, well-ordered town, and for a time the State Capital of Massachusetts. Today it attracts, from all over the world, visitors who come to step ashore on the carefully-preserved stone on which the Pilgrim Fathers first set foot in the New World, a few days before Christmas in the year 1620.

A Tomahawk

A Bow Case
and Quiver

A Birch Bark
Tepee

A War
Club

A Moccasin

A
Cradle
Board

A Birch Bark
Canoe

Indian Corn